Contents

Any words appearing in the text in bold, **like this**, are explained in the glossary.

Henry – eight and great?

Henry is a favourite name for kings of England. Eight kings have had the name, but none since 1547, when Henry VIII died. Perhaps the eighth King Henry was so famous – or thought to be such a monster – that no later king wanted to be compared to him. Henry VIII is famous as the king who had six wives. He was a member of the Tudor family. The Tudors did much to make England a powerful nation, and gave their name to an age.

Violent times

As a young prince, Henry was admired for his many talents. As king, he made England a force to be reckoned with in Europe. As an old, sick man, grown fat and frightening, he was feared.

Henry lived in a violent age. Sending two wives to have their heads chopped off seems terrible to us, but in Tudor times, no one was very shocked. For most of his life, Henry had one aim. He wanted to hand on his crown to a strong son. A strong Tudor did eventually follow in his footsteps – not a son, but Henry's daughter, Elizabeth, the greatest of all the Tudor rulers of England.

◄ This painting is by the Dutch artist Joos van Cleve. Henry looks as if he expects to be obeyed, and he was. In Henry's time, a king had more power than any prime minister or president today.

How do we know?

We know a lot about Henry. Paintings show him looking fierce, dignified and proud. Books and government documents tell of Henry's marriages, his wars, and the people who advised him. Ruined English abbeys remind us of his quarrel with the **Catholic** Church. Many places that Henry knew, such as Hampton Court Palace and Deal Castle, can still be visited today.

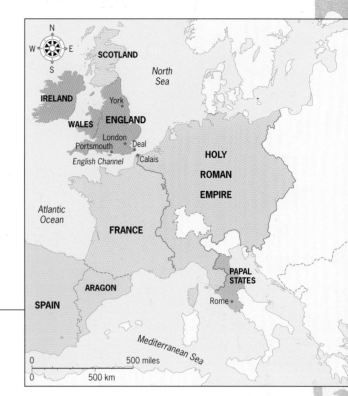

▶ Tudor England was not as strong as France or Spain, but it was growing stronger. Scotland had its own king. Wales and Ireland were ruled by Henry.

Who were the Tudors?

Tudor was Henry's family name. The Tudors had a claim to the throne of England because Henry's grandmother, Margaret Beaufort, had royal blood. Her father, Owen Tudor (1400–61), married Queen Catherine, who had been married before to King Henry V.

Key dates

1491	Henry is born at Greenwich, near London
1509	Henry VIII becomes king and marries Catherine of Aragon
1533	Henry marries Anne Boleyn
1534	Henry breaks with the Church in Rome
1536	Henry marries Jane Seymour. Wales and England are united
1537	Henry at last has a son, Prince Edward
1540	Henry marries Anne of Cleves, and then Catherine Howard
1543	Henry marries Catherine Parr
1547	Henry dies in London

Peace after civil war

Henry was born in a country recovering from bloody **civil wars**. For 30 years, two powerful **noble** families, called York and Lancaster, had fought to rule England. The York soldiers wore a white rose as their badge, the Lancastrians a red rose. So these wars are called the Wars of the Roses. The last battle was fought at Bosworth in Leicestershire in 1485. King Richard III (York) lost and was killed. Henry Tudor (Lancaster) won, and became king as Henry VII.

A second son

The new king married Elizabeth of York. By this marriage, he hoped to end the hatred between the two families. A son, Prince Arthur, was born in 1486, and a second son, named Henry, was born at Greenwich on June 28, 1491.

Prince Henry was born into an exciting age. The **Middle Ages** were ending, and the new ideas of the **Renaissance** were spreading. In 1492, a new world was discovered beyond the Atlantic Ocean when Christopher Columbus sailed from Spain to the West Indies.

◄ Paintings of Henry's father, King Henry VII, show an anxious-looking man. The king was watchful, hard-working and careful with money.

◀ This early 16th-century drawing by an unknown artist shows Henry VIII as a young child. His father was relieved to have two sons. A king needed sons to rule after him.

Rebellion threatens the Tudors

The king's delight in his second son was cut short by news of a **rebellion**. The rebels claimed that a young man named Perkin Warbeck was England's real king. The rebellion rumbled on for eight years until Warbeck's death in 1499. Few rulers in Europe thought the Tudors would last. As messengers hurried in with news of battles and arrests, Henry would have realized a king had many enemies.

Claims to the throne

Enemies of the Tudors twice tried to make someone else king. In 1487 they backed an unsuccessful revolt led by Lambert Simnel. A bigger danger came from Perkin Warbeck. He pretended to be Prince Richard, one of the two sons of Edward IV. They had died in the **Tower of London** in 1483.

Young Henry's England

Henry spent most of his childhood in the royal palaces in London, by far England's biggest city. His father was often away, visiting the **nobles**, whose soldiers he needed to guard his kingdom.

The lives of ordinary people

Ordinary people knew little about the quarrels of their rulers. News travelled slowly. William Caxton had begun printing books in London in 1476, but books were still rare and there were no newspapers.

Most people lived in small villages, and seldom travelled further than the nearest market town. Many were farmers, living in thatched cottages with one or two rooms. Farm records tell of houses and barns 'in a very ruinous state', and even of houses falling down! Villages and towns were dirty and smelly, with open ditches for drains. Homeless people begged by the roadside.

▲ Henry was taught by a private teacher. There were some town schools for boys, like the one shown here, painted in 1482.

Henry's world

Henry saw nothing of this world. The people he met at **court** were nobles and merchants, seeking the king's favour, and priests of the **Catholic** Church.

As a boy, Henry expected people to obey him. His father was the king, and above everyone else in England. Even a prince had to do lessons! His 'scolemaster' was the court poet, John Skelton, a clever man who could read Latin and Greek.

Henry was a bright student. He wrote poetry, and played the harp and the lute. He was probably always ready to slip away and ride his pony, or watch the **falconers** training their hawks.

▶ Girls did not normally go to school. They helped at home. This picture shows women doing the washing.

A hard life for most children

Tudor children were lucky to grow up at all. Six out of ten children died as babies or from childhood diseases. Lucky to be healthy, well fed and sleeping in a warm bed, Henry was also fortunate to have an education. Few children from ordinary families went to school.

Weddings and funerals

In 1501, Henry's brother, Prince Arthur, married Catherine of Aragon, a Spanish princess. King Henry VII was delighted, hoping that the marriage would bring friendship with Spain. Dancers, jugglers and tumblers entertained the Spanish visitors.

Henry's prospects change

In April 1502, Arthur became ill and died. At ten, Prince Henry faced the future. One day he would be king. Anxious to keep Catherine's marriage-gift, or **dowry**, Henry VII wrote to tell the King of Spain that his younger son would marry her, as soon as he was old enough.

For the next seven years, Henry learned the ways of kingship. In 1509, his father died. He was worn out by the cares of ruling, but left a fortune collected from taxes. He died confident that Henry would make a strong king, for the young and energetic prince already seemed more popular than his father had ever been.

▶ This 16th-century portrait is of Catherine of Aragon. She and Henry were happy for the first few years of their life together.

The new young king

Henry was just seventeen when he became king. The tall, red-haired prince cut a handsome figure riding through London, and the crowds cheered him. Perhaps now England would enjoy peace. Thomas More, Henry's friend and adviser, looked forward to 'an end of sadness, the beginning of joy'.

Six weeks after he became king, Henry married Catherine, as his dying father had wished. She was 23. Some churchmen said it was not lawful to marry his brother's **widow**, but the **Pope** in Rome gave Henry permission. A new reign had begun well.

▶ Henry as a young man, painted in 1509. Europe's rulers heard good reports of England's new king, who seemed to be able to do most things well.

The Tudors at table

There was much feasting to celebrate Henry's marriage and coronation. Rich Tudors ate a lot of meat – beef, pork, **mutton**, **venison**, and wild birds. Spices helped to give a better flavour. A banquet ended with pastries, cakes, jellies and fruit, washed down with ale, cider and wine.

The ideal ruler

Henry appeared to be the 'ideal ruler' that **Renaissance** writers described. He was clever, he spoke four languages, he loved music and poetry. For the first two years of his reign, he enjoyed himself hugely being king – showing off on horseback, **jousting** like a **knight** of old, dancing and eating too much at banquets.

▲ This picture shows Henry jousting in 1512. Queen Catherine watches from the stands.

The king must have a son

Life in Tudor England hung by a thread. Death, from one of many diseases, could strike even a healthy young man, like Henry. The king needed a son who would be king after him. Catherine gave birth to six children between 1510 and 1518. Two were sons, but only one child, Mary (born in 1516) survived. The deaths of these babies cast a cloud over Henry's marriage.

Running the country

Henry was content to leave the everyday business of government to others. He was lazy, unlike his father, who had rarely stopped working. Henry thought writing was a bore. He preferred to hunt deer and wild boar, play tennis, practise his skill with a knight's lance and write songs.

He wanted to be popular, so he sacked his father's tax-gatherers, even though this meant he got less money. Henry was content to choose a clever man to be his chief **minister** and let him run things, so long as the results were good. If not, the minister must watch out! He relied more and more on England's most crafty churchman, Thomas Wolsey, to run the country.

▼ These men are playing the game of real (royal) tennis. The young Henry was a keen tennis player.

The Renaissance

The **Renaissance** ('rebirth') was a time of change and discovery. Beginning in Italy in the 1400s, new ideas about art and science spread all over Europe, helped by the new **printing press**. Explorers such as Christopher Columbus set out to cross the oceans. The young Henry was interested in this wider world.

The quest for glory

Henry was keen to play his part on the European stage, and saw a chance to win fame by going to war. He decided to challenge England's old enemy, France.

Henry goes to war

In 1513, a fleet of ships carried Henry and his army across the English Channel to France. It was not a big war. Henry captured two French towns, and won a small battle.

King James IV of Scotland was a friend of France, even though he was Henry's brother-in-law. He saw the chance to make trouble and invaded northern England. This was a mistake. An English army beat the Scots at the battle of Flodden, and among the 10,000 Scots killed was King James himself.

The French war ended in a peace agreement, worked out by Wolsey. The war cost a lot of money, but Henry did not mind. He had shown his courage on the battlefield, and could now claim to be one of Europe's greatest kings.

▲ Henry sailed for France on the ship named in his honour, nicknamed the 'Great Harry'. It was the pride of his navy.

▲ This 16th-century painting shows the famous meeting of kings at the Field of Cloth-of-gold in 1520. Henry is on horseback, surrounded by his **courtiers**.

The Field of Cloth-of-gold

In the summer of 1520, Henry set sail in his splendid new warship, *Henry Grâce à Dieu* (known as the 'Great Harry'). He crossed to France, to make friends with the French king, Francis I.

The two kings set up camps near Calais. There were 2800 tents for the followers of the two kings. There were fluttering banners, music, **knights** in gleaming armour and feasting. Nothing like it had been seen since the **Middle Ages**. The meeting of the two kings on the 'Field of Cloth-of-gold' was talked about across Europe.

Living like a king

Henry enjoyed spending the money that his father had collected in taxes. His clothes sparkled with rubies and diamonds. He also loved new palaces. Wolsey, another big spender, built the finest palace in England at Hampton Court. This made Henry so jealous that Wolsey gave him the palace as a present.

Advising the king

Thomas Wolsey was the son of butcher. He had entered the **Catholic** Church and risen to a high position, becoming **chaplain** to Henry's father. He had known Henry VIII since Henry was a boy.

Wolsey runs the show

Henry was happy to let Wolsey govern England, and in return he helped Wolsey to rise higher in the church. He persuaded the **Pope** to make Wolsey **archbishop** of York in 1514. Then in 1515 Wolsey was made a **cardinal**, a 'prince' of the Catholic Church. As England's **Lord Chancellor**, Cardinal Wolsey was second only to the king.

Wolsey was clever, but greedy. He used his power to make himself very rich. He demanded new taxes, which people did not like. England's **nobles** hated Wolsey, who they feared would take away their old powers. Henry did not trust any noble. He insisted that nobles at **court** must eat dinner with him, so that he could keep an eye on them.

▲ Hampton Court Palace was given to Henry by Wolsey, who had spent a fortune building it. It had 280 beds for guests.

Henry and the Church

Henry had no time for Church reformers either. When a German monk, called Martin Luther, began asking for changes in the Catholic Church, Henry wrote a book attacking him. The Pope rewarded Henry with the title *Fidei Defensor*, Latin for 'Defender of the Faith'. The letters 'FD' still appear by the head of the **monarch** on British coins.

▶ This 16th-century portrait of Wolsey shows him in the red robe of a cardinal. He was an ambitious man, who hoped he might be the next Pope.

Reforming the Church

The Catholic Church had fallen into bad habits. In 1517, Martin Luther protested about them by nailing a list of complaints to a church door in Germany. This was the start of the **Protestant** movement for change, known as the **Reformation**. Soon there were Protestants in England, too.

A son, a son!

By the late 1520s, Queen Catherine was over 40, and Henry feared she might not have more children. He was desperate for a son, to be king after him. Henry had an **illegitimate** son, Henry Fitzroy, but Fitzroy could never be king. What was to be done?

Henry called his **nobles** to his new London palace of Bridewell, and told them he was unhappy about his marriage to Catherine. Possibly it had not been lawful after all to marry his brother's **widow**, and for this God had punished him by denying him a son.

A second marriage

Henry had his eyes on a new queen. He had fallen in love with Anne Boleyn, one of the ladies of the **court**. He wanted Anne for his wife, but first he had to divorce Catherine. Divorce was not as simple as it is today. The **Pope** had to rule that Henry's marriage to Catherine had never been a proper marriage at all.

Wolsey's downfall

The Pope refused to do this. Henry was furious and blamed Wolsey. Wolsey was arrested for **treason**, but he fell ill, and died in 1530 before Henry could have his head cut off.

◄ This picture shows Thomas More with his family. He is on the left, wearing a chain on his black robes. More was a lawyer and a scholar, one of the cleverest men in England, and a faithful Catholic.

► This 16-century portrait is of Thomas Cromwell. Cromwell had been Wolsey's assistant. He was a businessman and **moneylender**.

Henry chose two new **ministers**, Thomas Cromwell and Thomas More, and told them to arrange his divorce. Henry had known Thomas More for 20 years and greatly admired him. Together they had strolled in More's garden at Chelsea, gazing at the stars and talking of many things.

Kings, Queens and marriages

Royal marriages were usually arranged, to make friendships between countries. Henry's daughter, Princess Mary, expected to marry a foreign prince or an English noble. Wives were supposed to obey their husbands. If Mary became queen, her husband would rule as king. People in England did not like this idea.

Breaking the bonds

Thomas Cromwell suggested a way to solve the king's marriage problem. Henry could make himself 'govenor' of the Church in England, separate from the **Catholic** Church. Then the **Pope** in Rome could not stop Henry marrying again. Henry agreed, and so did **Parliament**, but Thomas More would not agree.

Henry remarries

In January 1533, Henry married Anne Boleyn in secret. In May, the king's marriage to Catherine of Aragon was declared 'never to have happened' by Thomas Cranmer, the new **archbishop** of Canterbury.

Queen Anne travelled by boat up the River Thames to London, escorted by fire-eaters dressed as devils. Henry met her at the **Tower**, kissing her in front of a crowd curious to see their new Queen.

▲ A portrait of Anne Boleyn, painted in the 16th century by an unknown English artist. Anne was dark-eyed and, unusually, had a sixth finger on her left hand.

Henry takes the Church's money

Anne's first child was a daughter, Elizabeth, born in September 1533. Henry hoped for a son next time. Meanwhile he told Cromwell to end the power of the Church in England, and bring in some much-needed money at the same time.

Cromwell set about closing **monasteries** and seizing Church lands. Church gold poured into Henry's treasure chests. In Churches, the services and the Bibles were now in English. The **Catholic** Church used Latin.

Thomas More bravely refused to swear the **oath** agreeing that Henry was now govenor of the Church in England. It was the end of their friendship. More was tried for **treason** and beheaded on the **block** in 1535.

◄ In 1536, aged 45, Henry had himself painted by Hans Holbein. The king admired Holbein's skill. He told a nobleman, 'Remember, of seven peasants I can make seven lords, but not one Holbein.'

The end of England's monasteries

Cromwell's men stripped England's monasteries of their treasures, including the lead from their roofs. They drove out the monks and nuns. Great abbeys, like Fountains Abbey in Yorkshire, still stand in ruins as reminders of Henry's 'dissolution' of the monasteries.

Three queens depart

Queen Catherine, who had been sent away from court, died in January 1536. By the end of May, her successor, Queen Anne, was also dead.

Anne goes to her death

Anne failed to give Henry the son he wanted so badly. She became pregnant for a second time, but a baby boy was born dead. Henry turned on her, accusing her of seeing other men secretly. She was shut up in the grim **Tower of London**, and sentenced to death for **treason**.

Nobles were usually beheaded with an axe, but Anne asked to die by a sword. An executioner was brought specially from France, to kill her swiftly. The men who had been accused with her were also executed. Two-year-old Princess Elizabeth was left motherless.

▲ Tudor gardens, like this one at Hampton Court Palace, were laid out in a formal way, with paths and flowerbeds 'framed' by hedges. The Tudors loved flowers and also surprises, like hidden fountains.

Henry's third queen

Two weeks later, Henry married again. His new queen was Jane Seymour, who had been a **lady-in-waiting** to Anne. Jane Seymour's two brothers, Edward and Thomas, were now important because of her marriage. At Henry's court, the rise of one noble family was always watched with envy.

In October 1537, to the king's great joy, Jane gave birth to a son. The baby, Prince Edward, lived, but Jane died twelve days after the birth. It was a cruel blow – Henry had his son, but had lost his queen. Now everyone watched and waited to see who would be Henry's next wife.

▲ Gentle Jane Seymour, shown here in a portrait by Hans Holbein, did her best to make the king friends with his elder daughter, Mary.

Gardens

Henry briefly enjoyed peace and contentment with Jane Seymour. The king and queen might stroll in their palace gardens, admiring the neat patterns of flowers and hedges and laughing as they became lost in the maze. Palace gardens supplied fruit and vegetables for the kitchen, herbs for medicines, and lavender to make rooms sweet-smelling.

Who dares to rebel?

Henry was growing older. After falling from his horse during a **joust**, he never fought in mock-battles again. He grew fat and complained of feeling unwell. His temper became even worse.

Rebellion in the north

Henry's son, Prince Edward, held the title of Prince of Wales. In 1536 Henry made Wales practically part of England, doing away with Welsh law. Official business had to be in English.

Henry was now likely to fly into a rage whenever he was not obeyed instantly. Anyone who opposed him risked prison or death. When **Catholics** in the north of England rose in **rebellion**, an uprising known as the Pilgrimage of Grace, Henry had the leaders executed.

Crime and punishment

In Henry's England, citizens going out after dark carried sticks or swords to fight off thieves. There was a lot of crime, even though punishments were harsh. A shopkeeper who cheated his customers might be locked in the **pillory**. Beggars were whipped out of towns. Prisoners were tortured to make them confess, and poor people were hanged for minor crimes, such as stealing chickens.

▶ Anyone locked in the pillory could expect little sympathy from the crowd, who often flung rubbish or stones at them.

◄ This portrait of Anne of Cleves by Hans Holbein persuaded Henry that she would be a suitable bride. After their divorce, Anne lived in England until her death in 1557.

A new wife

Cromwell suggested a new wife for the king. She was a German princess, Anne of Cleves, who was a **Protestant**. Marrying her would make Henry new friends among the German rulers. Henry admired a painting of her by Holbein, but when Anne came to England in 1540, he was disappointed and rudely said that she looked like a horse. They married, but were divorced soon afterwards, probably to Anne's relief.

Cromwell's fall

Henry felt that the marriage to Anne of Cleves had made him look a fool. He was angry, and blamed Cromwell, who was swiftly arrested. There was no trial. Abandoned by his master, Cromwell met the same fate as Thomas More, and was beheaded.

The last queens

Before the year 1540 was over, Henry had married again. His fifth queen was Catherine Howard, who was only about 20 – less than half his age.

Catherine was a **Catholic**, as Henry still claimed to be, despite his harsh treatment of the Church in England. She was pretty, but foolish. Her enemies soon whispered to Henry that she was flirting with young men, making a fool of him. That settled her fate. Catherine was beheaded in February 1542.

War with the French and Scots

Henry was always fearful of attack from Europe, especially from France. After all, the **Pope** had declared the English king an enemy, because of his treatment of the Church. To protect his kingdom, Henry built castles, such as Deal Castle in Kent, to defend the coast, and added new ships to England's navy.

Catholic Spain was still an ally. England and Spain fought France for three years, with little result except a steady drain on Henry's money. The Scots sided with France. In 1542 a battle at Solway Moss in the north of England ended with the Scots army beaten. Overcome with grief, the Scottish king, James V, died soon afterwards.

Guns replace spears

By the 1500s guns had become better weapons than spears and arrows. Henry had his own handguns. His ships had **cannons**, and in his new castles cannons were placed to fire from the walls. Henry encouraged English gun-makers to make more powerful guns.

VERA ET EXACTA
DELINEATIO CLASSIVM

Henry's sixth and last wife

In 1543, Henry married for the last time. His sixth queen was a widow, Catherine Parr. She looked after the king, now sick and so fat that he could hardly walk. She also brought to **court** all three of his children – Mary, Elizabeth and Edward.

Catherine gave them schooling and kindness.

▶ Henry VIII as an old man, in 1544. Once fit and healthy, the king was now an invalid, in pain and unable to walk without help.

▼ Deal Castle was built in under two years (1539–40). Its six round outer towers look like the petals of a rose – the Tudor symbol.

The England Henry left

In 1545, a French fleet attacked the Isle of Wight, off the South coast of England. English ships sailed out to give battle. King Henry had made the journey to Portsmouth and, from the shore, he saw the English ship *Mary Rose* roll over and sink. The French fleet was driven off, but at a terrible loss.

Henry's death

On 28 January 1547, the king died in London, at the age of 55. Henry's 9-year-old son became the next king, Edward VI. His reign was short. He fell ill in the winter of 1553 and died that summer. Then Henry's daughters Mary I (1553–58), a **Catholic**, and Elizabeth I (1558–1603), a **Protestant**, each reigned in turn.

▶ Elizabeth was like her father Henry in many ways. She was quick to learn, loved dancing, riding and hunting. She also expected to get her own way.

Henry's achievements

Henry fell short of his glittering early promise. His need for a son, and a divorce, led to a break with the Catholic Church that he probably never wanted. This helped to change England from a Catholic to a mainly Protestant country, perhaps more free to follow its own path than before.

Henry changed England more than he realized. The country got richer. New owners took over Church lands. English replaced Latin as the language of worship in churches. The **nobles** lost power, while **Parliament** and merchants grew stronger.

Henry's three children were the last Tudors to rule England. His daughter Elizabeth, red-haired and hot-tempered like her father, enjoyed a long and brilliant reign, but she died childless. In 1603, the English crown passed to King James VI of Scotland, and England and Scotland were united. That was a curious twist to the Tudor tale.

Return of the Mary Rose

The *Mary Rose* was built in the first years of Henry's reign, but rebuilt in 1536. Sailors thought it was a good ship, yet very few of the 700 men on board escaped when it sank so suddenly in 1545. The wreck was raised in 1982, and you can now visit the *Mary Rose* at a museum in Portsmouth.

▼ Divers brought up many objects from the *Mary Rose* wreck. This photo shows a key, a carved handle, cannon balls and other tools and equipment used by gunners. The ship tells a dramatic story of life in Henry's England.

Glossary

archbishop   chief bishop, or leader of the Christian Church

block   big piece of wood on which a person rested his or her head before the axeman cut it off

cannons   big metal guns that fired stones or metal balls

cardinal   senior bishop in the Catholic Church, chosen by the Pope

Catholic   member of a large group of Christians who obeyed the Pope in Rome

chaplain   churchman attached to a family or a school

civil wars   wars between different groups inside a country

court   a law court is a place where trials are held. A king's court was his palace and household.

dowry   gifts from a bride's family to her new husband

falconer   person who trains hawks and falcons for hunting

illegitimate   used to describe a child born to parents who are not married. In Henry's time, no illegitimate child could inherit from its parents.

jousting   form of sport in which one knight charged at another with a blunt-ended spear, or lance

knight   in the Middle Ages, a well-armed minor nobleman who brought footsoldiers to serve his lord or king

lady-in-waiting   noble woman who lived at the king's court, often as a companion to the queen

Lord Chancellor   chief adviser to England's king

Middle Ages   time in European history, roughly between AD 500 and 1500

minister   important government official

monarch   king or queen

monasteries   buildings where monks live

moneylender   person who lent money to others

mutton   meat from an adult sheep

nobles   people of high rank, with titles such as 'duke' or 'earl'. Nobles owned castles and lots of land.

oath   a solemn promise, usually made holding a Bible

Parliament   England's law-making body. In Henry's time, Parliament had less power than now. Its members (all men) met either in the House of Lords (nobles) or the House of Commons.

pillory   wooden frame into which a person was locked by the neck and wrists as a punishment

Pope   head of the Catholic Church. The Pope lives in Rome and in Henry's time was a powerful ruler.

printing press   machine for printing books from movable type

Protestant   supporter of the movement to reform the Cathlic Church, begun by Martin Luther, John Calvin and others

rebellion   uprising against a ruler

Reformation   religious reforms, or changes, in Europe which split the Western Churches

Renaissance   revival of old learning and spread of new ideas starting in the 1400s

Tower of London   fortress in London, used as a prison

treason   plotting harm against your own king or country, and so being a traitor. The punishment for treason was death.

venison   meat from a deer

widow   woman whose husband has died

Timeline

1485	Wars of the Roses end, Henry Tudor becomes King Henry VII
1491	Henry VIII is born on 28 June
1502	Henry's older brother, Arthur, dies
1509	Henry becomes king, and marries Catherine of Aragon
1516	Princess Mary born
1520	Henry meets King Francis I at the Field of Cloth-of-Gold
1526	William Tyndale publishes the first Bible written in English
1530	Cardinal Wolsey dies
1533	Henry marries Anne Boleyn. Princess Elizabeth is born
1534	Henry makes himself head of the Church in England
1535	Thomas More is executed
1536	Anne Boleyn is executed. Henry marries Jane Seymour.
1536–40	Monasteries in England are stripped of their wealth
1537	Prince Edward is born, Jane Seymour dies
1540	Henry marries Anne of Cleves and then Catherine Howard. Thomas Cromwell is executed.
1542	Catherine Howard is executed
1543	Henry marries Catherine Parr
1542–46	Henry goes to war with France and Scotland
1547	Henry dies in London on 28 January

Further reading & websites

Explore History: Tudor World, Haydn Middleton, Heinemann Library, 2001
On the Trail of the Tudors in Britain, Richard Wood, Franklyn Watts, 1999
The Tudor Court, Jane Shuter, Heinemann, 1998
Tudor Palaces and Other Great Palaces, Andrew Langley, Heinemann, 1997
The Tudors, Andrew Langley, Heinemann, 1997
Heinemann Explore – an online history resource.
 For Key Stage 2 history go to *www.heinemannexplore.com*
www.royal.gov.uk/history/henry.htm
www.maryrose.org

Places to visit

Mary Rose Museum, Portsmouth   Hampton Court Palace, Surrey
Tower of London, London

Index